# The New Times Nature Diary

# The New Times Nature Diary

Derwent May

Illustrated by Richard Blake

Robson Books

This Robson paperback edition first published in 1995. First published in Great Britain in 1993 by Robson Books Ltd, Bolsover House, 5-6 Clipstone Street, London W1P 8LE

**British Library Cataloguing in Publication Data**
A catalogue record for this title is available from the British Library

ISBN 0 86051 850 7 (hbk)
    0 86051 946 5 (pbk)

Printed in Great Britain by W.B.C. Book Manufacturers Ltd, Bridgend, Mid-Glamorgan, S. Wales

# Preface

Nature Notes by DJM first appeared in *The Times* on 11 July 1981. After a few erratic weeks, they settled down as a regular Monday morning feature, and have not missed a week since. They are always 200 words long, and were conceived as practical bulletins about what readers could see if they went out in the country that morning. They are not about a particular locality, but generally refer to what can be seen in the south of England, with regular forays to other parts of Britain like the east coast or the Scottish moors. Readers in the north usually find that birds are singing and wild flowers coming into bloom a week or more later – though there are exceptions like this year (1993) when the chaffinches were singing in Scotland before they began in the south.

This book is based on the Nature Notes, though the entries for each week are rather longer than the newspaper bulletins. Drawing on the records of the whole twelve years, they aim to give an unfolding portrait of a typical year. Every year is different, of course, so I have had to make certain decisions: I have given the year a short cold spell in January, a sunny spring, neither unduly early nor unduly late, and a fairly long, colourful autumn. Other years may prove better or worse. I have tried not to wax sentimental about nature in these notes, but sought to be vivid and precise in my descriptions.

My thanks to the Editor of *The Times* for allowing me to reprint them, and to my son, Orlando May, who put the manuscript on to the word processor, and edited it meticulously as he did so.

DERWENT MAY

# 1 January – 7 January

The mild New Year has set birds singing vigorously. Wood-pigeons take up their territories and coo regularly in the morning, though they flock again in thousands to roost at night. Song thrushes, wrens, robins and hedge-sparrows can be heard at any time of the day. There is a murmur of song occasionally from the goldfinch flocks, though many British goldfinches have left for France and Spain; those which remain feed from dead thistle-heads on the ground, or on the standing teasels in a damp corner of an allotment. They are the only finches with beaks long enough to reach the teasel seeds, which lie at the bottom of prickly tubes. Linnets produce their twangy song in a small chorus; they feed on the ground on the fallen seeds of persicaria.

Among the bare trees in parks and gardens, Algerian oaks still have bright green and yellow leaves on them. On the roadside, the pale green spikes of cuckoo pint are already several inches high, and unfolding to reveal themselves as arrow-shaped leaves. The heart-shaped leaves of jack-by-the-hedge, or garlic mustard, are also coming through, while small cow parsley leaves form thick carpets. Male buckler fern is battered but still green in the ditches. On dead tree stumps, candle-snuff fungus lifts its forked grey branches.

Otters are still active on streams and rivers; they go upstream at night to fish, or to catch an unwary rabbit or vole, then back to their lair in the river bank at dawn. Badgers should be asleep, deep underground, but a spell of weather like this brings them out to grub for a few acorns or beetles.

# 8 January – 14 January

Mistle thrushes are singing, a hectic trumpeting from the swaying tops of the trees. Black-headed gulls are showing the first traces of spring plumage, as the dark patch behind their eyes starts to spread into a facial mask. Herring gulls are courting and quarrelling in the sky: they stretch out their necks and emit wild, yelping cries. But winter immigration continues: this is the peak time for pochards, many of which have flown in from Russia. They are vigorous diving ducks, with red heads and grey backs.

Normally they live on large, shallow waters, where they can take seeds and vegetation from the mud at the bottom. Bearded tits from East Anglia or Holland are appearing in reed beds further west; they flit over the reeds for a moment with a pinging call, like a delicate glass being struck, then drop back into deep cover.

In low-lying pastures there are mixed flocks of jackdaws and common gulls. When alarmed they rise in a confused cloud, but quickly separate out. The black jackdaws wheel and dive low over the fields, their loud clacking cries sounding like a roar of applause, while the white gulls glide silently above them.

Snowdrops are out in sheltered spots; on river banks, the fragrant pink buds of winter heliotrope are opening. The leaves of Oxford ragwort are pushing up hard, and a few precocious plants are already in flower. Violet leaves are coming through in the woods; new ivy leaves have fine, pale veins. Earthworms are busy dragging dead leaves into their holes for food; blackbirds stand in line on a lawn, looking for the worms.

# 15 January – 21 January

Frost and snow drive birds to new feeding grounds. More tawny owls have come into the towns: they hoot and call all night as they search for sparrows roosting in the shrubberies. In this weather they can also be seen feeding by day. Short-eared owls move in from the east coast and are found beating up and down the river valleys. Redwings and fieldfares also flock westward; the redwing's thin note and the fieldfare's chuckling cry are heard in the treetops in city parks. Blackbirds and song thrushes scuffle among the leaves under the hedges where seeds and insects are still to be had. Unusual visitors come to well-stocked bird-tables: lesser redpolls, nuthatches and great spotted woodpeckers. Hunger is stronger than fear in many species, and robins venture in through open kitchen doors.

The loudest singers now are great tits, which can be heard even on very cold mornings if the air is still. Wrens are singing, but in a distinctly subdued way.

Wind blows the brown keys off the ash trees. Some of the sparse colour in the wintry fields comes from the white willow and the crack willow, whose young shoots are a pale olive-yellow. Water voles are normally nocturnal, but on very cold days they will come out of their holes to sit on river banks and feed in the sun. The small tortoiseshell butterflies that came out of hibernation in many places in the mild days of Christmas are now either dead or sleeping again in dark corners of garden sheds.

# 22 January – 28 January

The thaw may have come just in time to save the lives of many birds. But there have been serious losses. Mallard and tufted duck swimming in the last unfrozen corner of a pond have finally been frozen into the ice. Many redwings and fieldfares have been found dead or dying. Small birds find their food supplies barred to them: insect pupae in cracks in the bark are frozen over, slugs and springtails that live in the dead leaves are buried under snow, worms stay well below the hard surface of the ground. Coal and marsh tits often store seeds for the winter under moss or behind bark – but in these conditions they cannot get to them.

Waxwings have come in from Scandinavia: they roam about the countryside in search of rose-hips and cotoneaster berries, often in flocks. Long-tailed ducks from the Arctic have been feeding close in to the seashore on the east side of Britain: outside Edinburgh, on the Firth of Forth, they can be seen from the Corporation buses.

A few barren strawberries are in flower. Under weeping willows, the ground is strewn with silvery leaves, which did not fall until the snow came. On tree trunks, the powdery algae that live in the rain channels are jade-green in the sunlight. The crusty grey and yellow lichens also thrive in winter, when there are no leaves on the trees, and the light can get to them.

# 29 January – 4 February

Song thrushes have begun to sing again after the cold spell: their clear, flute-like notes, often repeated several times, are usually followed by some brief, muttered gabbling. Woodpigeons have also resumed their song, a gruff pattern of long and short coos that is never varied. They have also begun their soaring spring display flights. Some collared doves are heard singing even on the coldest days. Magpies are chattering around their old nests: they steer themselves through the branches with their very long tails, which swell out in the middle like a rubber pipe with a bulge in it. Greenfinches are calling with a long, slurping sound in the treetops; they will soon be in full song. Skylarks are singing over the meadows where lapwings are feeding among the growing grass.

In woods, winter aconites are coming into flower, though the petals do not open until the temperature is more than 10°C. The yellow flowers have a ruff of leaves beneath them. On hornbeam trees the long spiky buds are chequered brown and green, and yew trees have small yellow flower buds among the needles. Rosettes of dandelion leaves, like long green fishbones, are bursting out at the foot of walls.

Silverfish, which belong to a group of wingless insects called the bristle-tails, are active at night in kitchens and on open hearths. House-crickets are sometimes heard chirping in old buildings, but are much rarer than they used to be. Male winter moths are out flying when the evenings are mild and dry: they are pale brown with dark brown bands on their wings, and settle in a triangular shape. The almost wingless females live on orchard tree trunks.

# 5 February – 11 February

The first oystercatchers are returning to the Scottish moors from the western shores of England, but large flocks still remain on the estuaries, feeding mainly on cockles and mussels. They are large, black-and-white birds that fly fast, piping loudly, up and down the beach; and with their long, red beaks they can break their way into most shellfish.

Small parties of turnstones often feed near them, lifting the pebbles and the seaweed as they search for winkles. These birds will stay till April or May, then return to the high Arctic.

Jack snipe from the Arctic are feeding in the mud among low water plants. They have a remarkable habit of bouncing up and down, as if on springs, as they probe for food: the motion probably disturbs creatures in the mud and makes them easier to find. The jack snipe are usually solitary, but one or two common snipe sometimes feed near them: they are noticeably larger, and walk about steadily, while the jack snipe, its back curved and its head down, moves along like a bobbing beetle.

In the oak woods, jays are collecting the remaining acorns; on a sunny day they chase each other through the trees in a long line. Song thrushes are already prospecting for nesting sites in the bare hedges. Partridge coveys are breaking up, and the paired birds are settling in their territories.

In the West Country, some sweet violets are in flower, and their heart-shaped leaves are opening everywhere in the south. A few hawthorn bushes are showing small leaves: it is the same bushes that shoot early every year. By roadside ditches, the coarse, toothed leaves of hogweed are dominating the other spring growth.

# 12 February – 18 February

Blue tits are pairing. The two birds fly about excitedly, leapfrogging over each other in the twigs, with blue tits from neighbouring territories sometimes joining in the chase. Linnets are singing regularly again; the flocks are breaking up, and some mated pairs are returning to the gorse and bramble heaths where they will nest. Among the teal flocks, the drakes are challenging one another: they rise up in the water with their beaks bowed, then throw their heads sharply back. Meanwhile the females paddle restlessly around them, with thin, trilling quacks.

There are still many cormorants inland on lakes and rivers. Though they spend much of their time almost submerged under water, with only their heads and long beaks above the surface, they are also very competent perching birds. In the London Docklands, they land with ease on the tops of high cranes, and in some parts of Britain they roost in large numbers on suspension bridges. On the coast, gannets are returning to their breeding sites after a winter far out at sea: they sweep over the waves like giant gulls, their tails as sharply pointed as their beaks. They usually dive for fish at an angle to the sea, closing their wings just before they crash into the water.

Dark red flowers are opening on the bare twigs of the elm trees. On purple osiers by the riverside, silver catkins are opening: they have a reddish glow at the centre. On some crab-apple trees there are already a few pale green leaves, and young hornbeam buds are turning green. The first lesser celandines are in flower in sheltered places.

# 19 February – 25 February

Great crested grebes are back in full plumage, with dark ear-tufts and handsome chestnut ruffs. Their spring courtship displays are also beginning: the pair face each other on the water and waggle their heads with ear-tufts lifted and ruffs spread out. Between these head-shaking bouts, both of them engage in a ceremonial preening of their wings; when they move apart, they continue to call to each other with a sharp barking cry.

Chaffinches are singing again in most parts of the country. The male chaffinches have acquired bright blue heads and pink breasts; some are just trying out the first few notes of their song, some already have the full run of notes and the flourish at the end. Yellowhammers are singing in hedgerow trees; when approached, they flick their tails nervously and flit along the hedge tops. Their heads are primrose yellow. Some fieldfares have left for Holland and Sweden, but many are still feeding out in the middle of large fields; in the late afternoon, small flocks of them warble together in the treetops.

Snowdrops are growing in dense masses; they look like white waterfalls on the woodland banks. The three petals of the outer bell are now opening, and revealing the green-streaked inner petals. Some low-growing plants of wild angelica have gone on flowering throughout the winter; while on elder trees new buds are opening among the last traces of last year's leaves. Yellow catkins are swinging freely on the hazels.

# 26 February – 4 March

The noticeable new feature of the countryside is the blackbird song. The rich, leisurely fluting can be heard everywhere at dawn and dusk. It has an odd ventriloquial quality: sometimes it seems to come from the branches of a tree, but one looks for the singer in vain till he hops out from under some shrubs on the ground. Pairs of mallards are walking about awkwardly on the river banks, with the drake's head shining like green velvet; they are looking for safe nesting places under the hedges. On the east coast, winter migrants are beginning to leave: hen harriers that have been hawking on the marshes are drifting back to the Continent, Brent geese are deserting the estuaries and heading for Arctic islands.

More lesser celandines are coming into flower: the leaves lie flat on the ground and the buttery yellow stars stand above them. Flowers are growing thicker on the gorse bushes. There are new pink flowers on the red dead-nettles, and the first primroses are out. On crab-apples, the buds are like small crimson cherries, but will open to form white flowers.

Many badgers have come out of hibernation, and some of the sows are gathering moss and grass for that part of the underground set where the cubs will be born. Rabbits are already breeding. Frogs have practically disappeared from some eastern counties, but where they are still numerous they are gathering in ponds and pools to croak and mate. Some have already laid their jelly-like clumps of spawn.

# 5 March – 11 March

Flocks of redwings are singing in the treetops: a rambling, chattering song that has little resemblance to the true spring song that they will switch to when they return in the next few weeks to Sweden or Iceland. Soft calls, like lip-smacking, come from cypresses and gorse bushes where long-tailed tits are looking for nest sites. Lapwings are tumbling above the ploughed fields with plaintive cries. Coots collect pond weed from underwater but come to the surface to eat it: other coots often try to steal it. Now that the males are starting to compete for nesting places, there are more fights than ever.

On the moors, curlews are beginning their display flights: they rise steeply, but hang on quivering wings as their bubbling cry rings out faster and faster, then glide

down into the heather again. Lacking song perches in open country, this is their way of announcing that they own the territory around them.

The sallow trees are a mass of gold and silver catkins, and the first flowers, the colour of pure, pale white linen, are opening on the blackthorn bushes. Early wood anemones sprinkle the ground in dark woods: their six-petalled white stars are surrounded by fern-like leaves with a rich parsley smell. Daisies are multiplying on damp lawns, among lesser celandines that are already beginning to fade.

Male hares are starting to fight over mates: they rear up on their hind legs and box with each other, or jump over a rival and kick him from above. Bumble bees circle the new primroses, and bluebottles buzz against the window panes.

# 12 March – 18 March

Sparrow hawks are soaring over their territories, or calling with a shrill lamenting sound among the trees. This is the only time of year when they are so vocal and conspicuous; normally they glide silently along the woodland edges as they hunt for titmice and chaffinches.

Great spotted woodpeckers are drumming in loud bursts on dead branches. This is a warning to rivals not to enter the drummer's territory; but if one ventures in the occupant will attack it, flying up at it fiercely from below. Green woodpeckers do not usually drum, though they sometimes tap on a tree trunk when excited; they threaten intruders by ruffling up the red feathers on their crown, and rocking their head vigorously from side to side as they hang on the bark.

Reed buntings are beginning their jangling song in the osiers; the whole head is black in the males, apart from a white moustache and a white collar, and they have a rich chestnut-and-black mantle, like a fine rug. Goldcrests are singing in the conifers, a thin reeling song with a little explosion at the end of each phrase.

Dog's mercury grows in carpets in the woods; its tiny green flowers might easily be mistaken for seeds. Nearer the wood's edge, the first mauve flowers of ground ivy are coming out. The yellow colt's-foot is in flower on dusty roadsides, and the first marsh marigolds are opening by the streams. Vipers are coming out of hibernation, and black ants are on the move again. The first brimstone butterflies are careering along the woodland rides.

# 19 March – 25 March

Siskins are lingering in southern England because of the cold weather in the north. There are still plenty of seeds for these small, green finches in the black cones on the alders, where they hang upside down to extract them. Some of the males have started singing without waiting to return to their breeding territories: they have a thin, sweet song, with curious buzzing notes in it.

Many other birds are getting ready to nest. Kingfishers are inspecting holes in river banks; starlings are going in and out of holes in trees; coots are beginning to pluck at reeds, though not seriously starting to build yet. Drake Canada geese have a call that is almost like a song, a repeated set of rising and falling trumpet notes, uttered on the ground with head held high: when the pair flies up, their honking sounds like deep groans.

Wrens are singing higher in the trees and their song can be heard a quarter of a mile away. Chaffinches are singing energetically, and also making a distinctive call like a stone splashing into water. Little owls are yelping in the fields.

Everywhere hawthorn leaves are opening, in bunches like little green whisks. On the sallows, leaves are coming out on the twigs among the silver and gold catkins. On the black Italian poplars, there are brilliant red catkins, like fat caterpillars, which come tumbling down in the wind. On horse-chestnuts, the opening leaf buds are a pale papery green.

The first chiffchaffs are back from the Mediterranean: their clinking song rings out from the treetops. Newly arrived sand martins flutter and dart over lakes and rivers, where most of the early flying insects are to be found; they will not move on for another week or two to the sandy cliffs where they will make their nest holes.

Wheatears stop to feed on playing fields on their way to the rocky moors where they will breed; they are restless birds, bobbing, flicking their wings, and running fast to pick up an insect they have seen in the grass.

Shelduck are appearing on lakes and reservoirs as they

head back to the sandy coasts. They are like small black-and-white geese, with an orange band across the chest; the drakes have a bright red beak with a knob at the base. Mallards have begun nesting, and some are sitting on clutches of 11 or 12 olive-grey eggs.

Many hedges are a foaming white sea of blackthorn flowers; on some bushes the leaf buds are also opening. Other white spring flowers that are already out are greater stitchwort, cow parsley and wild strawberry. Dandelions are in flower everywhere, and in dry, stony places the lesser dandelion is to be found, with its smaller flower heads and sharp-toothed leaves. On sallow bushes the golden male catkins are now a decaying mass of threads, while the fertilized female catkins are long and green.

## 2 April – 8 April

Millions of willow warblers and sedge warblers that have been making their way up through France are poised to invade Britain. Willow warblers are very similar in appearance to the chiffchaffs that were arriving last week, but they have red legs, not black, and their song is unmistakable: a rippling cadence of notes like water trickling over a rock. The sedge warblers are furtive birds that sing from thick bushes at the edge of ponds and ditches – a babbling song, in which sweet notes alternate pell-mell with harsh, grating sounds.

In lambing fields, mixed flocks of magpies, jackdaws, rooks, and woodpigeons gather to feed around the sheep. In the woods, cock pheasants press their tails on the earth and flap their coppery wings, as they send their explosive trumpet-calls over the dry bracken. Moorhen are fighting on the ponds, rearing up and striking at each other with their green feet. Starlings and house sparrows stuff their beaks with white feathers as they begin to nest.

The half-open leaves on the horse-chestnuts are like small green parachutes; some have already been blown down by the wind. Forsythia has woven itself into some hawthorn hedges, and its spiky yellow flowers mingle with the bright green shoots. Bulbous buttercups are opening in the meadows, and goldilocks – the only woodland buttercup – in copses and under hedges. On still or slow-flowing water, the pale white flowers of water crowfoot tremble just above the floating leaves. Grey squirrels are beginning to mate; when they are alarmed on the ground they move off in a cautious series of bounds and motionless tableaux.

Blackcaps dart energetically through the treetops, singing every time they pause with a sustained rich jangle of harsh and melodious notes. Rooks, long-tailed tits, song thrushes and hedge sparrows all have eggs in the nest. Usually the hen bird lays one egg a day until the clutch is complete, and then begins incubating. A hard frost may addle the unattended eggs of an incomplete clutch, but once incubation has begun the eggs are not so likely to be affected by cold weather, as the female only leaves the nest to feed for very short periods. In the case of rooks, the male actually brings food to the female on the nest; while the domed nest of the long-tailed tit gets extra heating at night, when the male comes inside to roost on top of the female.

Over the lakes where tufted duck are gathering, a sweet, musical murmur is heard from the drakes courting the brown females. The last of the wintering teal are going north to the moors.

The second wave of trees is coming into leaf after the horse-chestnuts and hawthorns: there are small translucent leaves on the limes, there is a sprinkling of leaves along the elm twigs, and the pink sycamore buds are bursting. The silver birch woods are dusted with pale green. Stubby plants of yellow Oxford ragwort are coming into flower on the roadside. Stinging nettles are ankle-high, often growing among goose-grass and red dead-nettle.

# 16 April – 22 April

Cuckoos are back, calling tirelessly across the fields. Nightingales sing in the copses by day and night. But not all singers in the dark are nightingales: robins and wrens can also be heard in the small hours. Carrion crows have eggs in their conspicuous treetop nests; the male keeps the female company, and feeds her with large insects while she incubates. Woodpigeons sit among the cherry blossoms, and peck at the sprouting leaves: they often tumble off the thin twigs. On the Suffolk lagoons, avocets are back. They became extinct in Britain in 1844, but since 1947 they have slowly established themselves again. They are noisy black-and-white birds that scoop the water from side to side with long, upturned bills. On marshes and moors, red-shanks are trilling and yodelling.

White wood anemones carpet the sunny banks; wood-sorrel crowds around the tree stumps in shady beech-woods. The first bluebells are opening among their long, slender leaves. Bugle is appearing on the roadside, its powder-blue flowers half-hidden by its purplish leaves. Wood-spurge grows thick in southern woodlands; it has bright green cups with smaller, stemmed cups rising out of them. The watery lilac blossoms of cuckoo-flower, or lady's smock, are waving on long stems in damp meadows. On the river banks, horsetails are pushing up through the grass: they look like spiky brown thimbles on top of a pink stem.

On sunny woodland edges, speckled wood butterflies have emerged. They have a flickering, erratic flight, and are often first noticed because of their shadows on the ground.

# 23 April – 29 April

More nesting is under way. Blackbirds and song thrushes are on eggs in their deep nests, with just their beaks and tails showing above the rim. They sit tight, but fly off with a skittering cry if an intruder comes too close. Wrens are building: the cock bird makes several domed nests of grass and leaves, and the hen chooses one of them and lines it with soft feathers. She usually lays six minute, red-spotted eggs. New arrivals from the south include house-martins, wheeling and braking above the house tops and making a clicking note like a magic-lantern lecturer calling for his slides to be changed. The first grasshopper warblers are back: they have become much more common in neglected, bushy patches of countryside in the last few years. On the moors, blackcock gather for their annual 'lek;' a communal ritual of fighting and mating: the males spread their tails in a broad fan, and jump up and down in front of their rivals.

A few wrynecks are coming into south-east England. Although this bird is a woodpecker, it looks like a small striped thrush; it perches across a branch, continually twisting its head to look in every direction, then runs up a sloping bough and turns to sit across it. When it flies on, it flirts its tail in the air before settling once more. It draws attention to itself by its shrill call – 'ki-ki-ki-ki', like a very loud-voiced nuthatch.

Nearly all the trees are now coming into leaf. On the larches there are fresh green leaves and red female flowers. The new bright green leaves of the lime trees hang like small medallions, while on sycamores long flower spikes are already cascading under the leaves. On young hornbeams, the green turned-down leaves look like small birds' feet. In northern hedgerows bird-cherry is opening: this is a light, airy tree, with widely spaced branches on which feathery fingers will soon appear and turn into white blossom.

# 30 April – 6 May

Swallows are back around the barns where they will nest: the males chase each other in the sky, sometimes swerving to pick up a fly while still in hot pursuit. The first wood warblers are arriving; they sing in the translucent green tops of the beeches, with a shivering call and an occasional trill like a nightingale's. Tree pipits are back, singing at the woodland edges and in parkland. They flutter up from a perch, then lift their wings and tail so that they look like shuttlecocks, and float down singing loudly until they are back on their perch again. Whitethroats have returned to the lanes; they also sing in the air, fluttering up from a hedge making their scratchy song, and dropping down jerkily as though they were on an elastic string.

Young coots are out on the water: they leave the nest three or four days after hatching, but return to it at night. They are quite unlike their parents, with bright orange heads and white-tipped beaks. Some robins are already feeding young in the nest. The first greenfinches are building in thick evergreens; the males are singing noisily, soaring through the sky on a wild, erratic course.

Under lime trees the ground is littered with pink bud scales as the luminous green leaves grow larger. Many horse-chestnut trees are in full leaf with pyramids of white flowers now opening on every branch. The pink and white blossom of the crab-apples is already falling in the rain. In the copses there are sheets of bluebells. The bell-shaped flowers of snake's-head fritillary nod in the wind in wet meadows and sometimes on damp lawns: some flowers are deep purple with flickering lighter patches, some are pale purple, some are almost pure white.

## 7 May – 13 May

The last summer visitors are coming in: swifts are screaming across the sky and garden warblers are singing deep in rhododendrons or honeysuckle. Flocks of sand-martins are digging out nest holes, wherever they can find undisturbed cliffs of sand or gravel. They buzz in front of the cliff face like brown insects. Whinchats have arrived on the moors; they bob on top of the gorse bushes, with short bursts of song like a rapid robin. A few pairs of marsh harriers are back on the Suffolk coast: they sweep across the reed beds on massive wings, suddenly turning and pouncing on a frog or a moorhen.

Olive-green oak leaves are coming out, with catkins dangling by them: among the catkins there can sometimes be found what looks like a redcurrant, which is the home of the grub of a gall-making wasp called the spangle gall. A wedge of crinkled leaves and catkins is breaking out of the thin, spiky buds of the beech trees, and the bronze bud-scales flutter to the ground.

Fragrant white flowers are opening on the rowans, but like hawthorn flowers they have an acrid smell mingled with their sweetness. Fields of oilseed rape are a sheet of yellow flowers, with the buzz of honeybees coming from every part of it. Cowslips are abundant in some meadows. Holly blue butterflies are out in the woods: when they settle they show their distinctive silvery underwings. A common moth just now is the silvery-brown brindled beauty; its twig-like caterpillars are also appearing on apple trees and willows. Black ants are exploring gaps under larder doors.

# 14 May – 20 May

Turtle doves have returned from tropical Africa; they sing their purring song deep in the blackthorn hedges. Spotted flycatchers that wintered in the same regions as the turtle doves are back in gardens and churchyards; their thin song is seldom heard, but they are conspicuous as they dart into the air for an insect, then swoop back to the wall or tombstone on which they were perching.

In town and country, the air is full of blackbird song, especially towards evening: a lazy-sounding song of a few rich, fluting notes followed by a tired whisper. It can be drowned by the calls of young starlings that have now left the nest and fly after their parents from tree to tree begging to be fed.

White and green are now the prevailing colours in the countryside, as more hawthorns come into flower, spreading their scent far around them, and the cow parsley grows thick and tall. There are also small rosettes of white flowers on the wayfaring trees. The last of the trees have come into leaf: ash trees have spiky shoots of new leaves between the crimson flowers, while plane trees have young leaves tinged with bronze. There is a moment in mid-May when the foliage of the trees is at its fullest and freshest green.

The untidy pink flowers of ragged robin are in bloom in wet meadows while on dry roadsides mallow is opening. The tall spotted orchids are coming out here and there in southern England; early purple orchids, with their smell of tom-cats, are already common throughout most of Britain. Three species of white butterfly are on the wing: the large and small cabbage whites, and the dainty green-veined white. Ragged-looking comma butterflies settle on sunny hedges; common blues flutter restlessly over heathland.

# 21 May – 27 May

Blackbirds and song thrushes are still singing vigorously; a male blackbird will sometimes sing with his beak full of insects on his way to feed his young. Green woodpeckers are nesting; they bore a new hole in a tree each year, a foot or more deep, and lay their translucent eggs on woodchips at the bottom.

Ringed plovers are nesting on shingle beaches: they have four blotchy eggs arranged like a cross in a hollow. Near them, solitary bar-tailed godwits feed in the shallow water: these are birds who have left it too late to go up to the Arctic to breed, and will have a lazy summer in Britain.

On the black Italian poplars, the young leaves glitter like copper in the sun. Horse-chestnuts are already like hills of darkening foliage and white blossom. In limestone country, the spurred purple flowers of the wild columbine are appearing. Wild grasses are growing tall, with meadow foxtail grass already three feet high and its silky spikes dipping in the wind. In meadows where cuckoo-flower is blooming, there are many delicate orange-tip butterflies.

Caterpillars of the gold-tail moth are common on hawthorn hedges. They are red, black and white, with poisonous spines; the moth they will turn into is pure white, with a golden tuft at the stern. Fox cubs are out of their earths, and playing above the ground; the vixen will stay with them till autumn.

# 28 May – 3 June

On the moors, female cuckoos sit on walls and bushes, looking out for meadow pipits' nests in the grass. During the afternoon, the cuckoo will glide down to a pipit's nest, remove an egg, and lay one of her own in its place. Her offspring will later throw out the other eggs, and any nestlings that have hatched before it. Most cuckoos lay about a dozen interloping eggs in a season.

In the Outer Hebrides, corncrakes are back; until the grass and corn grow taller, they stay in the beds of yellow-iris leaves, climbing up on stones to make their loud, grating call resound over the islands. Great northern divers are still making their way up western coasts: at high tide they come in closer to the shore, where their massive bills and brilliant spangled backs can be clearly seen. Oyster-catchers are displaying excitedly on the rocks: they point their long red bills downwards and pipe loudly to drive an intruder away. A few are already nesting in shallow scoops in the meadow grass.

Bluebells are dying, and the first petals are falling from the snowy hawthorn bushes. After blackthorn in April and hawthorn in May, the third white flower to dominate the hedgerows is the dog-rose: early individuals are already coming out, and they will be at their best by the middle of June. They have large, floppy petals, often flushed with pink. The meadows are full of buttercups; red campion is already tall in the woods and on chalky hillsides the wayfaring trees are a dense mass of woolly green leaves and creamy flower-rosettes.

# 4 June – 10 June

Birds are at all stages of nesting. Most of these summer broods, hidden in deep foliage, will survive, though the rain has washed out the nests of some blackbirds and song thrushes. Garden warblers and blackcaps are sitting on their mottled eggs in loose, grassy nests, usually in brambles or honeysuckle. There are bright green young in the domed nests of the willow warblers – they crouch on a soft bed made of two or three hundred feathers, sometimes with their tails in the entrance. The adult willow warblers will try to lure a cat or human away, calling with a pleading note, and trailing a wing as if it were broken.

Young blue tits are calling from their nests deep inside lamp posts. Rooks have already fledged, and young and old fly in circles, cawing, high above the rookery. Young carrion crows are out in the fields; they hop heavily after their parents, still expecting to be fed. Lapwing chicks turn up their tails and bury their beaks in the grass when their parents fly overhead, giving the alarm: the young birds are richly mottled to match their surroundings, but when they run their white collars are conspicuous.

Many June flowers are already abundant. Poppies and ox-eye daisies are thick in the grass. In the cow parsley family, or umbellifers, pignut is out; it is distinguished by its sparse, spiky leaflets just under the white flowerhead. Yellow rocket grows in big clumps on the banks of rivers. The first cat's-ears are opening – solitary dandelion-like heads on a long bare stalk.

Red deer calves call plaintively for their mothers while they are still dark-furred and wet, lying at the foot of a tree. But they will soon be running in their dappled coats with the hinds.

# 11 June – 17 June

On northern moors, dunlins are singing their high trilling song, like the vocal equivalent of shimmering heat. They sing both on the ground and in the air, and sometimes local skylarks imitate them very accurately. The neat nest of these small wading birds is hidden in a tussock of grass near water; once the young are fledged, they quickly return to the coast.

Snipe often breed on the same moors, though their range extends to boggy places throughout the south of England as well. They are also aerial performers – not singing, but diving down with their outer tail feathers spread to produce a bleating noise as the air rushes through them. Whinchats nesting on the moors make sharp, scolding noises on the tops of the gorse bushes as they wait to take food to their young.

Honeysuckle is in bloom, smelling sweetest in the twilight; after it has been pollinated by moths, its white or pink flowers turn orange. Bugle covers the woodland floor with misty blue patches; in the shadiest parts of the wood, yellow pimpernel is in flower. On chalk hills there are fragrant orchids which have a long purple spike of flowers, and pyramidal orchids which are more tent-shaped, with a disagreeable smell. On lime trees, flower buds are growing out of the papery wings that will eventually carry the seeds away: the little cluster of knobs on stalks looks like the model of a molecule. The first meadow brown butterflies are flying along roadsides, the males chocolate-coloured, the females predominantly orange.

# 18 June – 24 June

Birds have a busy, preoccupied air; most of them are feeding hungry nestlings or fledgelings. Finches have begun a second brood: goldfinches build again in the swaying outer branches of fruit trees, linnets in thick bramble hedges. Tawny owls range far at night to gather mice and beetles, and are heard hooting in unexpected gardens. The young owls in the nest hole pipe loudly, sometimes beginning to call even before they have broken out of the egg. The robin's song begins to falter; the wren's voice dominates the countryside.

Midsummer flowers are out in profusion. Greater stitchwort sprinkles the ground with white among the young bracken plants; it will die as the bracken canopy closes over it. The purple flowers of tufted vetch twine round the grasses; grass vetchling, with its long thin leaves, is almost undetectable in the meadows, until its deep crimson flower opens on the stem. Poppies and ox-eye daisies fall with the first hay. On woodsides there are tall stands of pink foxglove. Deeper beneath the trees, there are starry white clusters of sanicle.

Water crowfoot covers the ditches with flowers and leaves. Yellow flag stands in clumps on the lakesides; out in the water, yellow water lilies stick up at odd angles on their stems, like the head and neck of some small lake monster. On beech trees the last dry nutshells of last autumn tremble and fall, while the new fruit swells, green and hairy, on the same twig. In cornfields, harvest mice have young in their nests, which are beautifully woven balls of grass, suspended between the stalks.

# 25 June – 1 July

Oak woods are full of blue tit and great tit families, feeding on the caterpillars. Sometimes a blue tit will haul up a dangling caterpillar by its own silk thread. Young cuckoos are out of the nest, but still pursuing their foster-parents with loud chirpings; when they have been fed, they often peck at the robin or meadow pipit that has adopted them. The adult cuckoos are silent, and lead a solitary life in the treetops; in a month they will be gone.

Young downy white gannets are growing in their nests on island cliffs, but some will die from a new hazard. The nests are usually made of seaweed, but gannets also pick up coloured nylon threads from fishing nets and weave it in with the other material. Subsequently it gets tangled round the legs of both nestlings and adults. In the Channel Islands, winter sorties have been made by helicopter to remove the tons of nylon on the ledges. Shags are nesting in similar rocky places; the pale brown nestlings put their heads right down their parents' throats to feed. The adult shags are already losing the curly black tuft on their crown that gives them their name.

Most duck are going into 'eclipse', when the brightly coloured males look more like the females. Drake shovelers lose all their brilliant green, white and chestnut and turn into a muddy purple; drake pintails lose their fine neck pattern. They will all resume their distinctive plumage in the autumn.

Giant hogweed is in some places ten foot high, and in recent years has often formed populous colonies. These small forests are dangerous, since touching the plant in sunlight brings up blisters. The first blossoms are appearing on brambles and attracting crowds of butterflies. Red flowers hang from the stems of many stinging nettles, and dogwood flowers have opened in the hedges. Stoat families hunt in packs and take many young rabbits.

# 2 July – 8 July

Skylarks are still nesting in the corn: many females are sitting on a second clutch of eggs, while the males sing high overhead. When they come down to ground and run along a field path, they look like small game-birds; when they skim over the waving barley, with their long wings and hesitant wing-beat they seem like brown swallows.

Corn buntings are singing in hedgerow trees or on electricity cables over the fields: they have a short, jangling song, which they deliver with head thrown back and thick beak open wide, as if they were snarling. Some males have several mates, and survey their various nests from their high vantage-point, without helping the females with the nestlings.

At field-edges, the first scabious flowers are opening: they are like jewelled mauve pincushions. Nipplewort is in flower: its small yellow blossoms close quickly when the sun goes in. Hedge bedstraw is coming out everywhere, with its innumerable tiny stars: sometimes it is like a thin mist in the grass, sometimes it grows in large, creamy-looking masses. In chalky places, the ragged purple flowers of greater knapweed are abundant and almost always have a bee sipping at them. There are still a few seedheads of goat's-beard on the roadsides: they look like crystal globes, and when they break up the seeds float away on large parachutes.

Ringlet butterflies are just emerging: they are chocolate-coloured above, but when they settle on bramble or thyme they close their wings and patiently allow an observer to see a line of ringed eye spots on their underwings. Frothy blobs of cuckoo-spit are seen on many plants, especially privet and goose-grass: inside each capsule of foam is a green spittlebug nymph, feeding on the sap.

# 9 July – 15 July

Young magpies already have tails as long as their parents', and are very pugnacious: they will run at a flock of pigeons and send them flying. But they still beg for food, calling harshly and fluttering their wings. Goldfinches come down on to railway lines to eat the seeds of the Oxford ragwort growing between the rails. House-martins fly tirelessly round the roof-tops; the glossy-blue parent birds have been joined by the juveniles, who have a distinctly browner tinge. All the family roosts in the small mud nest at night. Collared doves are still soaring and gliding in sexual display, but it is a rather half-hearted performance compared with the bold and noisy soaring and swooping of the woodpigeons. On northern moors, twites are nesting in the heather or gorse: they are like small grey linnets with pale bills, and the male has a pink rump. They fly as fast as linnets, singing as they go.

The ground is sticky under the lime trees: the minute aphids that feed on the leaves coat them with a honey-dew that slowly drips off. Ladybirds come to the limes to feed on the aphids and bees come for the rich nectar in the flowers. Under horse-chestnut trees, the grass is covered with embryo fruit that has been knocked off by the thunderstorms. Three spectacular wild flowers are just coming out: nettle-leaved bellflower with its white buds and spiky violet trumpets, and the two finest willowherbs – rosebay willowherb in pale pink spires, and great hairy willowherb, or 'codlins and cream', in purple-pink clumps that are often six feet tall.

Painted lady butterflies have come up from the Mediterranean: they fly in sweeping zigzags along the lanes, then settle on a sunny patch of ground and fan their white-streaked orange wings.

# 16 July – 22 July

Birds lie on their sides and rest in very hot weather: a black-bird has been seen lying with its head resting on a small stone. In gardens, the noisiest birds are families of spotted flycatchers; they call continually with a sharp, high-pitched note as they dart through the top branches of the limes and ash trees to snap up flying insects. The first waders are beginning to come down from the north and are appearing on the estuaries. Greenshank step delicately along the edge of muddy pools on their long green legs; when they fly up, they give a triple, yodelling cry. Whimbrel sometimes feed near them. Common sandpipers bob at the edge of lakes and streams, then fly off across the water on flickering wings. Little ringed plovers gather in deserted gravel pits, where they run rapidly across the sandbanks.

Most trees are now a much darker green, and leaves are withering in the drought on some horse-chestnuts. But on rowan trees fresh green leaves are sprouting at the end of the shoots, as the berries turn scarlet. On oak trees, the acorns are growing plump, but are still hard and green.

Hedge woundwort and stinging nettles grow over the woodland paths. The purple flowerheads of lesser knapweed or hardheads attract small skipper butterflies, which rest with their rear wings flat and their orange forewings held upright.

Two plants which have yellow flowers on spikes are now common: the sweet-scented great mullein, which has thick, downy grey leaves, and agrimony which is shorter and more wiry. Long beak-like seed-pods are appearing among the electric blue flowers of meadow crane's-bill. In sunny places the first blackberries are ripe.

# 23 July – 29 July

Most summer bird song is coming to an end; but skylarks are still singing high above the ripening wheat, and the yellowhammer's song chimes on through the long, hot afternoons. Goldfinch families are very noticeable in the trees; they all have flashing gold wing-bars, and the parents have a shining red, white and black face. Robins look worn and battered with the effort of feeding their young, who can be heard hissing deep in the hedges.

The flowers of high summer are in full bloom everywhere. By the roadside, there are tall mallows, bushes of hedge bedstraw and the yellow ladders of melilot. Dry, chalky places are overgrown with the dark yellow flowers of St John's wort and pale pink centaury. Rosebay willowherb makes patches of shocking pink among the bracken. The soft young heads of teasel are guarded by a ring of curved silver spears. The petals of the dog roses have fallen, but green hips are swelling beneath the star-shaped sepals.

There are thick clusters of flowers by the edge of ponds: the handsome purple spires of marsh woundwort, tall clumps of great hairy willowherb, and low tangles of white and pink yarrow. Chicory grows in dry places, its misty blue flowers lined all the way up the long stalk; the large yellow flowers of bristly oxtongue open among the prickly, white-wealed leaves. Black-and-orange caterpillars of the cinnabar moth strip the ragwort plants almost bare.

# 30 July – 5 August

Some birds are still tending their young. On grassy heaths, meadow pipits make an insistent call like a cricket chirping, as they wait nervously to take food to their nestlings; a few females are still incubating a late clutch of mottled chocolate-brown eggs. Around the Scottish coasts, eider-duck are swimming with flotillas of ducklings; they make a noisy party, with the females continually grunting and growling, and the young piping shrilly. Puffins are feeding their solitary nestlings, deep in sandy burrows; if the mouth of the burrow collapses, the adults whirr the sand out in a brown cloud. Fulmars also have a single chick in their cliffside nests. The parents fish out at sea, gliding on stiff wings; when they come back, the cliffs echo with murmurs and rattling cries from the nests.

The nut-shaped yellow flowers of hop trefoil are common in the long grass. Tufted vetch already has black seed pods, which reveal a silver lining when they split open. The greenish-white flowers of traveller's joy are sprawling over the hedges. Wild basil, which has bright pink flowers and faintly aromatic leaves, is common under hedges; and in some chalky lanes there are banks of lesser calamint, a small, pale purple flower that sends waves of fragrance across the road. Wild carrot is out at the edge of fields: it has flowers like small white saucers, with a tangle of feathery bracts beneath them.

Spindle trees are showing small green seeds which look like four-pointed club-heads; whitish-green hazel nuts are fattening in their leafy sockets, but they will not be ripe for a month or more. Conkers are swelling in their spiky green cases.

# 6 August – 12 August

Most of the barley has been harvested, and where the stubble is being ploughed flocks of black-headed gulls are foraging in the newly turned earth. The first wheat is being cut, and house sparrows come into the fields to pick up split grain. Kestrels have finished breeding; the young birds swell the numbers hunting along the motorway verges.

On the Scottish moors, families of red grouse are joining up in small parties; when they rise from the heather they give a cackling cry, and whirr into the distance, tilting from side to side. On Scottish coasts, more curlews are coming down to feed along the shoreline; and in sheltered pools behind the sand-spits there are often quite large gatherings of red-breasted mergansers.

Foxglove is abundant. On the moors it grows with the yellow tormentil; lower down it is found with rosebay willowherb and red campion. In the west of England, the small white spires of wall pennywort stand among their round leaves in shady lanes, and English stonecrop, with its starry white petals and red stems, grows among the rocks where the sheep feed. Cow-wheat is common at the shady edges of oak woods: its lipped yellow flowers all face the same way on the stalk, and it feeds on the roots of trees and other plants. Bilberries are ripening everywhere on the hillsides; some are already fat and juicy.

Young frogs have dispersed and are foraging for insects in the thick grass, but they will return to their native ponds to breed next spring.

# 13 August – 19 August

Yellow wagtails have finished nesting in the fields, and begin to flock together in reed-beds at dusk. They will soon be leaving for west Africa. Swifts career in wild screaming-parties round roofs and steeples: on a cool morning, with a favourable wind, they will suddenly disappear, bound for South Africa. Lapwings are beginning to arrive from the Continent: the first flocks consist mainly of young birds who have set off ahead of their parents.

Herons still stand on their nests, though their young are fully grown and can only be distinguished by their grey heads and rudimentary crests. Sometimes a flock will set off to feed together; they call to each other with a duck-like quack, rather than the usual deep honk of a solitary bird. Starlings wheel in the air like swallows, in pursuit of flying ants. Blackbirds are moulting: they look like worn velvet cushions.

Yellow toadflax is bright on the roadsides; lilac flowers are appearing on the burdocks. Wild strawberries can be picked in dry woods. The drooping purple cones of buddleia are found growing wild on railway embankments and waste land: they attract enormous crowds of in-sects, especially peacock and small tortoiseshell butterflies, bumblebees, and drone flies, which are a long-tongued species of hoverfly. Other kinds of hoverfly (of which there are over 200 varieties) are busy feeding in the convolvulus, or licking up the honeydew left by aphids on the leaves of flowers. Yellow underwing moths flash their lower wings as they fly along a hedge, but vanish when they settle, their dull upper wings merging with the twigs and leaves.

# 20 August – 26 August

The first robins are singing again as they take up their autumn territories. This autumn song is thinner and less varied than the spring song which begins at the end of December. As well as the males, some females are now establishing territories, but they will abandon them and join up with a male in the new year. Great tits are also singing intermittently: in these late summer days there is often a short burst of aggression and competition before the tits join up in their winter feeding flocks.

Jays occasionally produce a curious song, muted screams mixed with magpie-like chattering and musical notes. Collared doves are still singing energetically on television aerials in village high streets. On coastal mudflats, shelducks are fussily escorting their broods of ten or twelve young. The grey-capped juveniles, almost as big as their parents, walk in a long line; the two parents, honking nervously, walk either side of them.

Burnet saxifrage is in bloom: this is one of the most delicate of the 'umbrella' flowers, and is distinguished by the very small leaves at the top of the stalk and the large ones at the bottom. Tansy is out, with its button-like yellow flowers and lemon scent. Dry grass is everywhere dotted with small dandelion-like flowers: this is autumnal hawkbit, which has a rosette of small jagged leaves at its base. Most hawthorn berries are still apple-green, but some have a dark-red flush.

Gatekeeper butterflies chase each other over marjoram and knapweed; wall browns settle on dry paths. On downland by the coast, grayling butterflies are on the wing. When they alight, they close their dappled orange wings, and tilt them towards the sun, so that they do not cast a shadow by which predators might detect them.

# 27 August – 2 September

Swallows are gathering in twittering flocks on telephone wires or the warm tiles of farm buildings; sometimes they all fly up from the roof in an obscure panic, but quickly return again. After a few days of excitement like this they set off on migration for South Africa.

Sedge and reed warblers have deserted the lakesides and ditches; tree pipits have left the woodland edges. Willow warblers are moving south on a broad front. All these species are now *en route* for tropical Africa, with thousands crossing the English Channel every day. Chiffchaffs are also leaving, but most of them will go no further than the Mediterranean – and they will be among the first spring migrants to return next year, at the end of March.

On many lime trees, a whole branch is turning yellow, while the rest of the tree remains quite green; on the hornbeams, individual leaves are changing colour all over the tree, giving it a dappled look. Some birches have turned completely. Among the dead purple stalks of cow parsley, its dainty autumn relative, upright hedge parsley, is flourishing with many white and pink flowers. Badgers are busy extending their underground sets before the cold weather comes. Wasps are feeding on fallen fruit and jammy knives, but for the larvae in their nests they take back meatier food and can be seen biting off the wings and legs of a daddy-long-legs, or crane fly, before flying away with the body. On the moors, millions of bees are feeding on the heather, and produce a seamless humming that extends for miles.

# 3 September – 9 September

Curlews are at the height of their migration on the shores and estuaries; both their ringing 'cur-lee' call and their bubbling summer trill are heard along the water's edge. Some house martins are moving south, but many can still be seen feeding out in the fields: they swoop over the heads of grazing cattle which have disturbed the insects in the grass. In the woods, mixed flocks of tits are forming: the coal tits are particularly noisy and active, hovering and darting among the twigs, and bursting into loud, plangent calls. The staccato whistling of nuthatches can be heard again, with one bird joining in after another until the treetops seem to be full of echoing typewriters. Great spotted woodpeckers are looking very bright after moulting, barred black and white above and scarlet under the tail; at this unhurried time of year for resident birds, they like to sit for long periods on the very pinnacle of a fir tree, looking around them.

Everywhere in the countryside there is a glimmer of autumn reds. Hawthorn bushes are laden with crimson berries, while the clusters of black elderberries are surrounded with vinous red leaves. On brambles, the ripening berries are a glossy red and some of the leaves are scarlet. The lower leaves of docks are also turning bright red. Rosebay willowherb is going to seed, and wasteland is covered with the white, fluffy spires. In the fields, much of the stubble has now been ploughed in; where it remains, grass, thistles, fat hen and scentless mayweed are all pushing up between the fading, yellow lines.

Brown aeshna dragonflies, the largest of the common dragonflies, dart and glide over the water, hunting until it is almost dark.

# 10 September – 16 September

Hobbies are small, scythe-winged hawks, that catch their prey on the wing; some are still at their nesting sites on heaths or lonely farmland, others are heading south catching house martins or dragonflies wherever they can. They fly very fast – now overhead, now far away, their plaintive calls fading.

On ploughed fields, there are small flocks of skylarks; and much larger flocks are starting to come in from the Continent. Many of the immigrants will move on to southern Europe, but the British skylarks will stay near their territories and resume song occasionally between now and Christmas. Meadow pipits are also arriving on the east coast. The pipits and the larks call as they fly, and can be heard passing through the sky at night almost anywhere in England. Whinchats are coming down both east and west coasts; they are quick, restless birds with a bold white eyestripe, which stop to feed in bushes in neglected fields. Eventually the whole European population will be settled for the winter in tropical Africa.

Leaves are yellowest on the elder trees. Limes, elms and horse-chestnuts are also beginning to turn. Many sycamore leaves are framed in brown. On hazel bushes, green nuts sit side by side with tiny, hard catkins that will dangle long and loose in the spring. There are black berries on the dogwood bushes, and yellow fruit litters the ground beneath crab-apple trees. Under oak trees there are many half-eaten acorns dropped by woodpigeons and grey squirrels. Small tortoiseshell butterflies are abundant; red admirals are starting to join the peacocks on the buddleias.

# 17 September – 23 September

Moorland birds on their way south are appearing in unexpected places; ring ousels – like blackbirds with a white gorget – stop to feed in the early morning on golf courses; merlins pursue skylarks and waders along the shore.

Great black-backed gulls from Norway are already well distributed along the east coast. They are enormous, fierce birds, and though they live largely on herrings, they have been known to kill lambs, cats and moles. They are mainly distinguished from lesser black-backed gulls by being larger, and by their white or pinkish legs. Lesser blackbacks, which have yellow legs, are only just beginning to come down from their northern breeding grounds. They are often found on fields inland when migrating; they roost on reservoirs and fly out in the half-light of dawn.

In marshy places the leaves of great water dock – up to a yard long – can still be seen. Water mint remains in flower and gives off a sweet scent when crushed under foot. The large pink flowerheads of hemp agrimony are looking grey and dusty as they turn to seed.

In damp fields, yellow flowers continue to bloom on silverweed, though its leaves are not as glittering as they were earlier in the year; and fleabane is still flowering abundantly. On heathland, harebells are still in bloom: they have long, spiky sepals at the base of the lilac flowers. They often grow near sweet-smelling mats of wild thyme, which also still has plenty of small pink flowers. The snapdragon-like flowers of yellow toadflax are abundant in grassy places; this is a tenacious plant, and if dug up can grow again from a small scrap of root left behind. Small heath butterflies are on the wing, mingling in some places with a late brood of meadow browns.

# 24 September – 30 September

Tree sparrows are flocking; the two sexes have the same plumage, like neat male house sparrows with a smudge on the cheek. Starlings are roosting communally again, both in dense woods and on city buildings. Most of these are British birds, but they will soon be joined by vast flocks of winter visitors from Germany and Poland. Wrynecks are now appearing in the eastern counties on their way south; they feed on the ground as well as in the treetops. Manx shearwaters have left their nesting holes and have spread all round the coast, where they skim with stiff wings over the waves. Practically all of them will move on to more southern waters. Kittiwakes are also appearing everywhere offshore; they are dainty gulls with a soft, dark eye, and will stay throughout the winter.

Some horse-chestnut trees have red or yellow crowns, though boys knocking down the conkers find that they are still white, or only streaked with glossy brown. Hawthorn trees also have many red patches, and Lombardy poplars are flecked with pale yellow. Golden rod is in flower on railway embankments; nipplewort is still common on roadsides, and daisies continue to open on lawns. In many places mushrooms and blackberries are at their best. Garden spiders are building large webs, which glitter when the morning mist collects in droplets on them. In the evening caddis flies swarm over ponds; there are almost 200 species in Britain, most with lacy wings and long thread-like antennae.

# *1 October – 7 October*

Teal are coming in from Germany and Denmark; they haunt the edges of lakes where there are reeds growing in the water. Sometimes they dabble, sometimes they swim a long way with their heads beneath the surface. The speculum on their wing is a glittering green; the drakes also have a comma-shaped green band across the eye. Snipe from the same part of Europe often feed near them on the mud: they probe deep with their long beaks, sucking up worms without raising their heads. Last chiffchaffs are singing in the sunshine, before they leave for the Mediterranean.

Conkers and horse-chestnut leaves are falling together, producing the first rich, musty smells of autumn. Lime and birch leaves are coming down in the wind. There are dangling green seed-pods among the pink flowers on Himalayan balsam: when the pods are touched they split open and leap in the air, sometimes two or three feet high, scattering the brown seeds. Wild Michaelmas daisies are found in extensive clumps on waste ground, looking like gigantic heather.

On garden walls, ivy-leaved toadflax is still in flower, and the yellow blooms of the ivy itself are full of nectar – the last feeding place of wasps and hoverflies before they die. The crackling leaves at the bottom of hedges are full of life, as slugs and snails go down from the branches, and ground beetles hunt for ants and the minute springtails. Female glow-worms shine at night: the winged males glimmer feebly. Late moths include the angle shades, whose fine green and chestnut markings blend with the dying leaves, and the merveille du jour, whose pale green wings match the lichen on the oak trunks.

# 8 October – 14 October

Fieldfares are back from the north of Europe: the first nervous one announces itself with a harsh chatter in the sky, then the surrounding hedges or treetops are seen to be full of them. Their blue-grey heads and rumps contrast strikingly with their chestnut backs. Black-headed gulls are now back inland in vast numbers; many of them roost at night on the reservoirs.

Young sparrow hawks are moving out of their parents' territories. They dart through the tops of the fir trees, snatching up small birds; sometimes they soar on rounded wings, surveying the land below. Buzzards are wandering afield; occasionally they pass over cities, very high in the sky. Kingfishers are leaving the rivers where they nested in the banks, and appearing on new waters. Blackbirds are gorging themselves on fallen apples. Apart from robins and wrens, there is little song: a brief outburst from a great tit or coal tit, the raucous cooing of a late collared dove. A few goldfinches and skylarks are also singing again – but this autumn burst of song will not last long.

There are thick drifts of yellow leaves under the black Italian poplars. Oaks and ash trees are still very green. The dry, white stalks of dead hemlock stand in clumps, with a few tall plants still bearing green leaves and white flowers. Wild angelica has large, dark brown seedheads; its shrivelling leaves retain their curious double form, with a fleshy bracket clasping the stem, and a second, fern-like leaf growing out of it.

# 15 October – 21 October

As autumn progresses, most birds are noisiest around dusk. House sparrows roost in huddled flocks in evergreens or under the roofs of houses, and chirp together loudly for up to an hour before they sleep. Blackbirds come to the edges of their territories and challenge each other with loud, chinking cries as the light fades; afterwards, if there is not much thick cover to be had, they too will gather together to roost. Hedge sparrows that have spent the day on their own call to each other with thin cries, and often roost in pairs. Robins generally sleep alone in fir trees or thick ivy.

Some young woodpigeons are only just leaving the nest, the last fledgelings of the year. They have white wing-bars like their parents, but not the white bar on the neck. A few woodpigeons are still singing, but they will not be heard regularly again until January. They have an almost invariable song of short and long cooing notes, which could be represented as 'Take two books with you, take two books with you, dolt' – the 'two books' being the most emphatic notes.

Hornbeams are rapidly losing their leaves, but on many the boughs are still crowded with hanging orange clusters of seeds, like frilly-edged lanterns. On ash trees there are patches of paler green or yellow, but most of the leaves will stay bright green until they fall.

There are bead-like streams of brilliant red berries where the black bryony has coiled round the stems of other plants or along wires; the leaves have often withered or gone. There are also shining red berries on the unrelated white bryony, which climbs with the help of small tendrils, not by twining itself round supports. The berries of both bryonies are very poisonous.

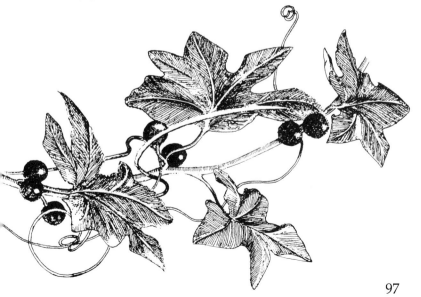

Pied wagtails are running about on farmhouse roofs, and occasionally singing on the crest; they have a short, babbling song, in which many of the sounds are like slurred, musical versions of their sharp call-note. Lesser redpolls are moving south and feeding on the catkins of silver birches: they sometimes send showers of the winged seeds floating down from the trees. Hen harriers are appearing on lonely marshes along the east coast: they sweep low over the land hunting for voles and snipe, and often sleep in small, communal roosts in reed-beds or long grass.

Most of the waders that come down the British coasts on their way further south have now passed through; those that remain will spend the winter here. They include up to half a million dunlin which have been coming in from Russia and Scandinavia (while the birds that bred on our own moors have left for Africa). The dunlin feed on the shoreline in large flocks; in flight, hundreds of them will twist and turn simultaneously at great speed and, as they land again, they all lift their wings high for a moment before settling down.

Leaves are showering down from the trees in the wind and scampering across open spaces, especially the large leaves of planes and Norway maples. Beech leaves are bronze and gold; they are mostly holding firm on the trees still. In the hedges, dogwood leaves are like purple smoke among the browns and greens; sometimes a nearby ditch is full of small dogwood saplings as well. Wild angelica is still in flower in damp places, its tall red stems swaying in the wind; there are also a few flowers left on yarrow and red clover.

# 29 October – 4 November

The last of the Arctic terns are passing along the coast: they dip through the mist, calling harshly. Some will go as far south as the Antarctic Circle. Golden plovers feed with the lapwings out on the arable fields. When they all rise, the lapwings spread out with slow, heavy wingbeats, but the golden plovers rapidly find each other, and the flock cuts sharply through the sky. Redwings from Scandinavia are back in Britain for the winter; they are like song thrushes with a bright red underwing which is very conspicuous when they fly up. Feeding on the berries in hawthorn hedges, they often use a call like the clucking note of blackbirds, but with a strong nasal twang to it; migrating overhead at night they utter long, thin cries. Song thrushes and mistle thrushes are singing again: some of the song thrushes sing more quietly than in the spring, but the mistle thrushes bugle as loud as ever from the swaying treetops.

On roadsides in the south, there is a late flowering of bristly oxtongue: every part of this plant is covered with rough hairs, except for the pale yellow flowerheads. Elm hedges are sprinkled with a brighter yellow, and oak leaves are shrivelling. Bracken is turning brown and gold. Beechnuts and sweet chestnuts litter the woodland floors, not yet hidden by fallen leaves.

In oak and beech woods, cep mushrooms, also known as penny-bun boletus, are growing large, with white flesh and sticky chestnut caps. Nearby there sometimes grows the brown-stalked bitter boletus. Money-spiders are on the move, floating through the air on threads of silk: on warm, dry days they sometimes descend in vast numbers on fields and gardens, covering the grass with their gauzy webs.

# 5 November – 11 November

Wild geese are back from their summer breeding-grounds in Greenland and the Arctic. They fly strongly in V-shaped skeins, different birds taking it in turn to lead. In England, the most commonly seen are white-fronted geese, with their conspicuous white faces; they roost on estuaries or floodwater, and fly in to feed on the clover and winter wheat. Pink-footed geese are commoner in the north; and on the west coast of Scotland, especially on the island of Islay, enormous flocks of the black-and-white barnacle goose come in, yapping like dogs. Brent geese are flocking into the estuaries of south-east England: they are smaller, darker birds, but also have a barking cry. They feed, mainly by day, on the long, green underwater ribbons of eel-grass.

In most parts of Britain, autumn leaves are now at their most spectacular. Beeches are ablaze with orange and yellow and the few remaining limes that have leaves appear like pale parchment lamps when the sun shines through them. Cherry and gean are in every shade of purple and crimson. Sweet chestnut leaves flutter through the air like slender yellow fish, while the last prickly seed-cases plop to the ground: the grey squirrels quickly clean out the chestnuts. A rich, musty smell of leaves fills woods and gardens.

On the downs, spindle-trees are colourful, with purple leaves and bright pink berries splitting open to reveal orange seeds. Many flowers linger in skimpy patches: ragwort, scentless mayweed, yellow toadflax, ground ivy. The white grass of late summer has vanished and the autumn grass is thick and green again. Pygmy and common shrews are found dead on paths and lawns: the adults die each year of exhaustion, and only the young are left to get through the winter in the hedge-bottoms.

# 12 November – 18 November

Kingfisher families have broken up, and the members have resumed their solitary lives. Though they are such brilliantly coloured birds, they are well camouflaged in waterside bushes just now, their blue backs and orange breasts blending with the green banks and red bramble leaves behind them.

Loud screeches in town gardens indicate that jays have come in from the countryside. They are a kind of pink crow; when perched, they show a thin blue line above their flanks, but when one sees them from an upstairs window, flying below, they reveal a large patch of brilliant blue on their wings. There are blackbirds everywhere: the summer population has now been swelled by many migrants from central Europe.

Misty yellows and oranges envelop the countryside. Pale yellow maple leaves glow with a luminous intensity, oak leaves wither from the edges. Guelder roses are like red columns, with their leaves pink or crimson and their berries a transparent scarlet. The yellow flowers of wild turnip are still in bloom here and there: it is like charlock, but with pointed leaves that clasp the stem. The straggling seeds of old man's beard look like patches of dirty snow on the hedges.

Adders and grass snakes have gone into hibernation, coiled under wood piles or in abandoned birds' nests in the heather.

# 19 November – 25 November

Lapwings, or green plovers, are feeding in flocks on ploughland, many of them winter visitors from Scandinavia and Germany. Black-headed gulls often stand among them, each marking a lapwing like a footballer: when the lapwing finds a morsel of food, the gull chases it with harsh screams until the lapwing drops it. The plovers will feed by moonlight to avoid these attacks.

On quiet lakes, there are now many shovelers and gadwall. These are surface-feeding ducks, unlike the tufted ducks and pochards which dive for their food. The drake shovelers are like tricolour flags floating on the water, with their green heads, white breasts and red flanks; both sexes have beaks like large, black shoe-horns, with which they scoop up plant seeds and water-beetles. Gadwall swim about in pairs, and spend much time up-ending: one often sees two of their barred black-and-white sterns protruding from the water side by side.

Leaves are thick on the ground. Some, like lime-tree leaves, disintegrate quickly; others, especially plane-tree leaves, remain firm and intact until well into the winter. Last wasps are coming into houses for warmth, but only the new queens will survive. Hedgehogs are making nests of leaves and moss to hibernate in, usually choosing a hole in a bank; sometimes they will use an old wasps' nest.

The tiny muntjac deer now found wild in much of southern England bark like a dog at night, and in these last days of autumn they are sometimes glimpsed among the crumpling purple bracken.

# 26 November – 2 December

Winter visitors are now more conspicuous in the bird population. On the coast, there are small flocks of snow buntings: their sandy plumage merges with the background until they fly up, but then their white wings and dancing flight make them look like whirling snowflakes.

On the east coast, there are a few Lapland buntings from the far north of Europe: they run like mice among the grass and sea asters at the edge of the shore.

The first bramblings from the north have also arrived; they are rather like chaffinches, to which they are closely related, but have bright orange shoulders and a white rump. They do not follow such regular migration routes as most birds, but each year seek out the districts or countries where there is the best harvest of beech-mast.

Young magpies that have not yet got a territory for themselves are roosting in small flocks. The older birds stay in pairs all through the winter, and remain in their territories. In cold weather they store acorns or other food in holes in the ground; while they are digging a hole with their beak, they keep the food concealed in a pouch under their tongue.

Flowers still to be found include Oxford ragwort and herb-robert, with pink blossoms and leaves. Teasel plants stand tall, some as much as seven foot high: their spiky, purple seed-heads are defended like the flowers were by criss-crossing white swords. On alder trees, new purple catkins are growing among the black seed-cones. Weeping willows are still quite green, but the remaining leaves on the oak trees have a grey washed-out look. Grass is still very green everywhere, and glitters in the low sun and the strong wind.

## 3 December – 9 December

Starlings are roosting in vast flocks in small woods or on city buildings. If they are disturbed at sunset, the roar of voices ceases and they fly up, to wheel and criss-cross in the sky; the moment they settle, their mass chatter begins again. Many individuals return night after night to exactly the same twig or cornice. Black-headed gulls leave the fields at dusk to roost on reservoirs or lagoons; they glide in circles high in the sky, the whole ring of them slowly drifting in the direction they want to go.

Goldeneyes are among the winter duck now appearing on inland waters: both sexes have shining yellow eyes, and the drake has a white cheek patch on his glossy green head. They ride low on the water and look rather deliquescent and shapeless. Female tufted ducks also have conspicuous yellow eyes, but they sit more trimly on the water than the female goldeneyes, and are a darker brown.

On frosty mornings, the clumps of dead rosebay willow-herb are like shining feathers stuck in the ground. A few winged seeds still hang on the sycamores, but they are too chipped and water-logged to spin down as they do in autumn. On osiers, the thin, drooping yellow leaves look from a distance like hazel catkins that are full of pollen three months too early.

Water rats, or water voles, are still active: they are heard more often than they are seen, as they dive with a loud splash into the water. After that, they return to a hole in the bank, or swim away well beneath the surface.

# 10 December – 16 December

The main autumn migrations are over, and birds have little to do except eat. But with the days so short they have to look for food almost continuously. A cold night will use all their reserves of fat. Canada geese go foraging in large flocks from lake to lake; when they up-end to feed in the water, the white feathers under their tails rise into the air like broad sails. Herons appear at garden ponds: they wade up to their thighs in search of fish, or stalk along the muddy edge and dive headlong when they see their prey. On the coast, wintering greenshanks walk in the shallow water and kick at the sand to bring food to the surface. Among the dead leaves blackbirds clear neat circles of bare earth where they can get at insects and worms. Bullfinches come down to the ground to feed on nettle and dock seeds, and any dried-up blackberries they can find.

Tawny owls hunt till dawn for mice and roosting sparrows and can sometimes still be heard calling well after sunrise. The long, quavering hoot is the male's song; the commonly heard 'tu-whit-tu-whoo' is in fact usually a joint performance, the female making the sharp cry and the male hooting in reply.

Weeping willows are the greenest trees left. Brambles still have many purple leaves on them; bracken is brown and broken. But next year's buds are already noticeable on many trees. On horse-chestnuts, the buds are dark and sticky, aspen buds are plump and pink and on beeches the sharp buds show through the clinging orange leaves. On oak trees, marble galls or oak-apples are conspicuous , now dry and brown and deserted by the gall-wasps which grew in them as grubs: the small hole in each shows where the wasp came out.

# 17 December – 23 December

In strong winds, unusual bird calls in the treetops generally prove to be creaking branches. The loudest bird sounds high in the trees at present are the sharp cry of the great spotted woodpecker and the chattering of magpies.

Woodcock are lurking beneath the bracken and the bramble in many woods. They are most often seen when a dog flushes them: they rise quickly, bursting through the foliage, and zigzag away through the trees. At dusk they usually leave the woods to feed on earthworms in damp fields or ditches: they probe with the tips of their bills, then sink them deep when they detect a worm. A common sound at dusk just now is the 'chissick' call of pied wagtails as they come with looping flight into their communal roosts in laurels or reed-beds, sometimes from five or six miles away.

Wintering swans are back in Britain. The smaller Bewick's swans are concentrated in the Ouse Washes and at Slimbridge, while whooper swans are found, sometimes on quite small waters, throughout the northern part of Britain. Both species have yellow bills, in contrast to the orange bill of the mute swan; they are often best distinguished from each other by their calls, the Bewick flocks baying like a pack of hounds, the whoopers trumpeting in the way their name suggests.

In neglected city gardens, feverfew continues in flower here and there, often nestling against a gatepost; and gallant soldier, with its tiny white and yellow flowers, rampages in the flower beds. In the afternoon, swarms of winter gnats dance in the air in sheltered places: these gnats belong to the daddy-long-legs family, not the mosquito family, and do not bite.

# 24 December – 31 December

On moonlit nights, and by well-lit roads and motorways, some robins start singing at three in the morning. They are often mistaken for nightingales; but all the European nightingales are in Africa by now, and will not be back until mid-April.

Siskins have come south again from Scotland and are feeding in the alder trees. They have a very soft twitter that can easily be missed; you look up and notice one, and suddenly see that the whole tree is twinkling with them, the breasts of the males like gold in the low winter sunlight. Sometimes a whole line of them is hanging head forward on a branch, like a line of quotation marks. On pines and firs, tree-creepers probe for insects under the thin bark: they leave a shower of reddish-brown flakes falling beneath them as they climb the trunk. Along the coast, stonechats have established their winter territories around gorse bushes, and spend most of their time feeding quietly on the ground.

Japanese autumn cherries are in flower; thick clusters of pale orange keys still hang on the ash trees; silvery seed-pods linger on the laburnums. In the tops of lime trees, gigantic balls of mistletoe covered with plump white berries sway among the red buds and twigs. Spruce firs are covered with long orange cones; they are shallow-rooted trees, easily toppled by the winter gales, and sometimes fall in a line like dominoes. (Most Christmas trees are young spruces.) Earthworms tug the dead leaves into their holes, eat them, and leave the remains on the grass as worm-casts. Seven-spot ladybirds come out of tangled vegetation into the winter sunshine.

# Index